All Aboard!

Written by Leon Rosselson
Illustrated by Scoular Anderson

Collins *Educational*
An imprint of HarperCollins*Publishers*

There once was a bus and the bus was red
And the driver sat inside
And goats galore galloped onto the bus
To go for a mystery ride.

And under the bus were the wheels of the bus
And the wheels were on the ground
And the wheels of the bus went round and around
And around and around and around.

And above the bus flew a gaggle of geese
And they honked to the driver inside
And the goats jumped up on their seats and waved,
Crying “Come with us for a ride.”

And under the bus were the wheels of the bus
And the wheels were on the ground
And the wheels of the bus went round and around
And around and around and around.

And next to the bus zoomed a buzz of bees
And they hummed to the driver inside
And the goats all stood on their heads and laughed
Crying “Come with us for a ride.”

And under the bus were the wheels of the bus
And the wheels were on the ground
And the wheels of the bus went round and around
And around and around and around.

And behind the bus raced a bounce of bulls
And they bellowed to the driver inside
And the goats got out their goat guitars
And sang "Come with us for a ride."

And under the bus were the wheels of the bus
And the wheels were on the ground
And the wheels of the bus went round and around
And around and around and around.

And the red bus tootled up a hill
And down the other side
And across a bridge which went over a stream
And the goats all laughed till they cried.

And under the bus were the wheels of the bus
And the wheels were on the ground
And the wheels of the bus went round and around
And around and around and around.

Then the red bus stopped where the land meets the sea
Which people call the seaside
And the driver yelled "All out of the bus!
It's the end of the mystery ride."

And under the bus were the wheels of the bus
And the wheels were on the ground
And the wheels stopped turning round and around
And around and around and around.

Then the goats played ball on the sun-washed sand
And danced by the waterside
Till the stars peeped out and the driver yelled
"It's time for the homeward ride."

And under the bus were the wheels of the bus
And the wheels were on the ground
And the wheels started turning round and around
And around and around and around.